5 Benefits of Worship

5 Benefits of Worship

Experiencing the Power of God Through Focused Praise and Worship

neville

Contents

Virtual Church Publishing

Toronto, Ontario, Canada

Cover design by Virtual Church Publishing

Cover copyright 2021 by Virtual Church Publishing

book (other than for review purposes), please contact us @ info@siloamministries.net. Thank you for your support of the author's rights.

All Scripture quotations in this book, except those noted otherwise are from the King James Version Bible.

Contact information

Email: info@siloamministries.net.

Company: Virtual Church Publishing a division of New Village Publishing and Communications

Website: www.nevillesolomon.com

Telephone: 416.996.5961

For additional information visit us @ the following...

Youtube.com Channel: Virtual Church TV Neville Solomon

Youtube.com Channel #2: Virtual Church Music Neville Solomon

Introduction

Hello and God bless, my name is Neville Solomon and I wanted to thank you for reading this book on "The Five Benefits of Worship." The book is focused on the purpose and power of worship. You will learn how to develop a positive and strong relationship with God and how to build the spiritual skill of worship. Worship is in fact the relational development of one's authentic connection with God through the skill of praise and worship.

As you grow in your knowledge of the Lord, you should also develop the spiritual discipline of praise and worship. It is my hope that you will learn a little bit more about worship through this book, and that it will help you to enhance your relationship with God as you make it a daily habit to lift up the name of the Lord.

If you are a committed follower of Christ, you may assume that your worship is fine and requires no changes. However, I would like to challenge you to see worship as a growing union with God. It is a divine experience that is partly relationship and skill. Since worship is both a relationship and a skill it can be enhanced and developed over time. In any relationship, intimacy and closeness are developed through spending time with each other. For this reason, you must spend time with God to grow your relationship with Him.

At times you may find it challenging to define what worship is? And for those who have a working definition of worship, you may find it difficult to make worship a practical part of your daily life. But I am confident that if you understand the importance of praise and worship and the great benefits associated with it. You will make it a priority to worship the Lord as much as you can.

This book seeks to provide an outline of five major benefits of worship, in an order that will motivate you to make worship a consistent habit. If you have been in church for years, or you are new to the subject of worship, I am confident that before you finish this book you will have an expanded view on the subject of worship and my prayer is that you will make worship a life-long, and daily practice.

Worship is a Spiritual Skill

Much like bible study, and prayer, worship is a spiritual skill. You may ask yourself; what is a spiritual skill? A spiritual skill is also known as a spiritual discipline, a habit, an exercise, or a practice that is a continuous activity that causes you to spiritually learn and grow over time. This growth implies to your personal relationship with God and your spiritual maturity. Much like a natural skill, a spiritual skill is an act of development through practice, repetition, and newly learned behaviours that create positive and productive results. The only difference is that a spiritual skill produces spiritual outcomes and a natural skill produces natural outcomes.

When you exercise your spiritual skill, you seek to build the muscles of your character and improve the cardiovascular fitness of your life with Christ. The purpose of a spiritual skill is to cultivate the practice of experiencing God's presence. It is important to set aside time for spiritual workouts that can train your soul. Spiritual skills are a necessary aspect of the Christian life. In order to grow spiritually, it is essential to be in fellowship with God and to allow the Holy Spirit to guide you. Consequently, the Holy Spirit also empowers you to be divinely transformed as you cannot grow without the Lord's help.

Although the Holy Spirit is the source of your spiritual growth, nevertheless, you are in partnership with God. Therefore, you must actively furnish the process of your spiritual development by giving your all in worship. There are four things that you can do to participate in the partnership with the Holy Spirit for your spiritual growth.

The first thing you can do is to have an authentic experience with God. An authentic experience with God is a practice that includes the following: By placing your faith in the unseen God, you create an atmosphere for spiritual growth. By the development of spiritual skills such as bible study, prayer, and worship that will enable you to flourish in your relationship and maturity in Christ. It is important to mention that there are countless spiritual skills that you must develop such as forgiveness, giving to the poor and sowing to the church, walking in joy, peace, faith, confidence, and a host of other spiritual skills that can be accessed through faith in the Lord.

The second thing you can do to enhance your spiritual development is to find a mentor, or a mature believer to guide you in your walk with God. It is important to allow godly counsel to be a part of your everyday life. The bible says, "Where no counsel is, the people fall: but in the multitude of counselors there is safety" (Proverbs 11:14). When I speak about having a mentor it doesn't mean that it has to be a formal relationship such as a pastor and a member. I just mean that you have some godly friends who are mature in Christ and can share their knowledge with you. I believe it is good to have several mentors, who can encourage your spiritual growth.

The third thing you can do to enhance your spiritual development is to pattern your spiritual life after historical models that have proved successful. The best people to model are those who have demonstrated the spiritual skills that you would like to grow in. I often find bible characters or great Christians in history as suitable models. In fairness, all of my models are people who lived and died in the faith because I am able to see how their decisions and actions worked out in their life.

The difference between mentors and models is that mentors share their perspectives with me and give me their different points of view. But models are those who have left a path that I can follow and get similar results from their life. You have a more complete understanding when looking at models because by comparing various historical characters you learn without having to experience the lesson yourself.

The fourth thing you can do to enhance your spiritual development is to repeat the process by using what you learned from mentors, and your models to have more informed experiences with God. The more you learn and grow in your relationship and revelation of God is the more teachable you become. A teachable person will learn better from mentors and models. When you learn from mentors and emulate successful models in your life, your experiences with God will become greater and greater. I would add that the Holy Spirit works within the processes where you learn through the instructions of mentors and experiences of models. Another term used to refer to the learning process from mentors and models is "discipleship." It is very important that you are taught and mentored by other believers.

It is important to mention that Christians who don't receive spiritual counsel and those who don't have models to emulate, generally struggle in their spiritual progress. I've met quite a few people who said they were Christians, but were lacking in integrity. Many of these individuals had strange biblical beliefs that stunted their spiritual growth and at the root of these issues were the fact that they had minimal personal experiences with God; no mentors, and no successful or biblical models.

I assume that you are not one of those Christians because you seek to learn by reading a book. Unteachable religious folk don't read, or listen to others. They don't attend church neither do they try to learn or grow because they feel they already know everything. Actually, I am of the opinion that they do watch strange YouTube videos and base all their beliefs on those, and don't get any teaching beyond that. Sorry, maybe they listen to the QAnon conspiracy theory teachings that are not grounded in reality. If you don't know what that is then you are truly blessed.

I suspect you may have met a Christian with some strange beliefs before. I met a bizarre man by the name of Bruce, who told me that he didn't believe, he needed anyone to teach him the bible. Bruce stressed that the Holy Spirit talks to him. He then he tried to teach me from the bible why his belief was true.

I asked him, "Why should I listen to you, if I only need the Holy Spirit to teach me?"

I made it clear that I didn't need him to teach me anything. Bruce then told me, "I'm an Apostle sent to teach the nations the bible." Crazy folk in the church! He doesn't believe that anyone can teach him, but believes that he is called to teach. That's arrogant and unintelligent.

I'm certain that if you have been in church for a while, you will meet strange people like this who call themselves Christians. However, if you haven't the best way to identify such immature individuals is to ask them what they have learned from someone else. If they speak about their experiences, but have never learned from anyone else, it is more than likely that they are one of these strange Christians and are not a growing and mature believer.

On one occasion, I asked Bruce who his mentors were and he said no one. He had a direct connection with God. I reminded Bruce that in the bible the people followed the Apostles' teachings (Acts 2:42). He then claimed he knew the bible better than the Apostles who wrote the scriptures themselves. Bruce further went on to emphasize that the apostles got a lot of things wrong in their christian journey and he knew more than all of them. When you have no mentors, models or personal experiences with God, all you have is confusion.

I will repeat that when I speak about learning from others, I don't mean having a formal mentor or even having a great pastor that you connect with regularly. What I am talking about is having a mature Christian or steadfast spiritual leader in the church that can help you with any questions you may have about the bible, that you currently don't understand. If possible, it is good to have numerous mentors or counsellors. Learning is vital part to developing spiritual skills and a part of learn is looking at issues from various angles, and adding their wisdom to your thought process.

You can usually find such support in your local

church or amongst your Christian friends. But if for some reason you find you don't have much support as a believer or you're just looking for additional support feel free to visit us at www.nevillesolomon.com and get in contact with us. Let us know if you have any specific questions from the scriptures or about prayer, worship, or the faith in general.

I would also add that along with having godly mentors it is important for you to have fellowship with other believers in general. "Not forsaking the assembling of ourselves together, as the manner of some is; but exhorting one another..." (Hebrews 10:25). When you assemble with other believers you have the opportunity to practice the three major spiritual skills of; bible study, prayer, and worship along with some other spiritual skills listed in the bible.

As mentioned earlier, personal experience, mentors, and models are essential to have a growing relationship with God. It's important that you spend time with God daily and make it a routine to work on the spiritual skills found in the scriptures.

It is vitally important to preserve intervals to study the bible, to pray, and to worship daily. Many call this practice having a "Quiet Time" with God. In order to grow in any skill, it is vital that you practice that skill and master it over time. If you want to learn more about developing a Quiet Time, please visit our channel at www.youtube.com @ Virtual Church TV – Neville Solomon (Quiet Time).

My Worship Experience

I learned that worship is a skill through my study of the word, and my experiences in worshipping God. I noticed that when I studied my bible repeatedly it changed me and I grew spiritually. The same is true when I prayed with passion on a consistent basis it changed me as well. Over my decades of experience in worship, I also noticed that consistent and persistent worship had radically altered who I am as a person. It is important to challenge yourself to praise God beyond your comfort zone. When you express your heart and soul in worship you grow spiritually.

I have also been blessed by numerous mentors in the area of worship and have learned so much from them. In the multitude of counselors, I learned how to worship God in spirit and in truth. Over the decades of my life, I have come to the conclusion that it is important to be teachable and to learn how to see things from different points of view. My Bishop taught me that you must put physical energy into your worship and cry out to God not only in spirit but in your body too.

My professor at the Toronto School of Theology (University of Toronto) taught me that theologically I was adopted into the family of God, my worship was sacred, and that it was a time of intimacy with my creator and I needed to set aside daily time to worship God and ensure that I connected with Him. I learned from my childhood choir director that worship meant nothing if God didn't show up, and that you could experience the presence of God if you opened your heart to Him.

My best friend Q taught me that worship was cool and that you can worship God in the presence of sinners. In high school, Q had a nice car with an even better sound system. I remember us pulling up into the school parking lot and he would have worship music blaring from his amazing sound system. He wasn't ashamed of his worship and this experience created the impression in me to value worship and never be ashamed to worship whether in the midst of the saved or unsaved.

I learned from my dear friend brother Silent that I was chosen by God to lead others into worship. Brother Silent really believed in me and would often let me know that I was gifted to worship and to share the word. These are just a few of the countless mentors that God has blessed me with. And if you are wondering, yes! My friend's name was Silent. That being said he was an outspoken man and was far from silent.

I have also had several biblical and historical models whom I emulate for worship. Individuals like Moses, Samuel, David, Daniel, Esther, Peter, and Paul have been significant models for my Christian life. There are numerous figures throughout history that have also helped to add to the growth of my worship experiences. Great revivalists like Martin Luther, John Wesley, William Seymour, Martin Luther King Jr., and so many others.

By studying the life of these great worshippers,' I have learned successful strategies for worship and I have understood the importance of obeying God. Worship is not simply giving God a sacrifice. Worship is a life of obedience to God. The biblical figure Samuel said it best when he said, "Has the Lord as great delight in burnt offerings and sacrifices, as in obeying the voice of the LORD? Behold, to obey is better than sacrifice and to hearken than the fat of rams. It is essential to hear God's voice and to obey what He says (I Samuel 15:22).

I have learned that if you are practicing the spiritual

skill of worship, you should see signs of spiritual growth. You should demonstrate the fruit of the spirit in your day-to-day life. This means you should be peaceful and loving in your attitude much like Christ. You should also see evidence of the development of essential spiritual skills such as bible study, prayer, faith, giving, love, and forgiveness. That simply means you should get better at the things of God such as understanding what the bible teaches and enjoying your time with God in prayer.

Worship helps you to grow, and the more you invest your life with God the more you will be blessed in the process. Worship has many benefits, and we will be exploring five major benefits of worship within this book. However, it is very important to make mention that the greatest benefit of worship is having a flourishing relationship with God.

The Skill of Bible Study

No one joins the church and fully understands the bible without studying and spending time in the word. In order to learn the word, you must undergo studying the bible either by reading the scriptures or listening to the word. When I was younger, I remember being so frustrated at times because my pastor knew the word so well, and with all my studying I couldn't understand as much he did.

In those days I used to pray and study, pray and study and beg God to aid me in understanding what the bible taught. In fairness, it took some time, but as the days went by, I grew in my spiritual skill of both bible study and prayer. I know the bible much better today and I love spending time with God in prayer, but it came over time as I spent quality time with God. In order to grow in the word you have to read the scriptures and learn from others.

For most people, their first experience with the word was through listening to a sermon at a local church. For others, their first experience of learning the word was through family members and home bible studies. Still, there are others who came into an experience of the word by listening to sermons on the radio or watching Christian TV. In working with men in prison, they mostly testified they came into a relationship with Jesus Christ by just reading the bible on their own.

As you mature in your Christian walk there comes a time that your development is based upon your own personal study in the Word. Once you get a solid understanding of the scriptures you are to invest time reading in order to allow the Holy Spirit to open your eyes to God's truths in the bible. Paul inspired his student Timothy by saying "Study to show yourself approved unto God, a workman that needs not to be ashamed, rightly dividing the word of truth," (2 Timothy 2:15). In other words, you need to spend time to build up the skill of studying the bible so you can understand God's Word.

I would add that you need to study the bible daily and develop a routine that includes reading the bible, writing notes in a journal of what you are learning, and reviewing those notes and what you have learned. It is important for you to understand what you are studying and to remember what you have studied so that you can exhibit what you have learned from the word in your life.

Another way to improve on the level of your personal bible study is by listening to tapes, watching online messages, and being a part of a small bible study group or a Sunday school class. It is also helpful to have friendships with mature Christians who can share their biblical wisdom with you. If you are fortunate to be a part of a local church assembly with good leadership you can also grow through church bible study and mentorship from the pastor.

As mentioned earlier, it is good to take notes of personal bible studies and also of sermons. I have many bible notebooks where I keep my notes, as well as some electronic notes on Microsoft Word. As time goes by, I am able to review these notes and they are such a blessing because I can review my notebooks and journals and see what I have learned over the years. I recently had the opportunity to review some of my mom's sermon notes and she was so blessed to be able to review what she learned over the years.

It is also good to create a plan of how you are going to apply the scriptures you have studied to your life. Putting that plan in your journal or a notebook is an excellent idea. Also sharing the plan with a friend or your mentor is another way to encourage yourself to follow through with making your bible study come alive.

For steadfast unwavering growth, it is very helpful to have godly spiritual leaders and mature Christians to support you in your journey of grasping the Word of God. The bible says, "How are you to hear without someone preaching? As it is written, how beautiful are the feet of those who preach the good news... So, faith comes by hearing and hearing by the Word of God" (Romans 10:14-15, 17).

The spiritual life has been designed by God so that we can learn from others within a community of believers on how to grow in a healthy manner, in our faith by the Word of God. The early church practiced this in that "They devoted themselves to the apostles' teaching," (Acts 2:42). As it relates to the word of God

Paul said, "All scripture is God-breathed and is useful for teaching, rebuking, correcting and training in righteousness, so that the servant of God may be thoroughly equipped for every good work," (2 Timothy 3:16-17 NIV).

Finding bible study models helps you learn the scriptures, and grow in your knowledge and practice of the word. Jesus is an excellent model for building intimacy with God. He woke up early each morning to spend time with God. He read the scriptures and based his daily decisions on the Word of God. Jesus said, "Man shall not live by bread alone, but by every word that proceedeth out of the mouth of God," (Matthew 4:4). It is quite helpful having a system of bible study that helps you to understand and live out the bible in your personal life. I try to model Moses, David, Paul, and Jesus' style of studying the Bible. I would add that your mentor can help you by sharing some of their biblical models for studying the bible.

The Skill of Prayer

Not only are you expected to grow in the discipline of studying your bible, but you are also expected to develop a consistent prayer life. As it relates to growth in the spiritual discipline of prayer, a person doesn't automatically learn how to pray. But, through consistent experiences of praying to a loving

God, and being mentored on an ongoing basis, by mature Christians, you can learn how to pray more effectively. In addition, if you model successful prayer warriors from the past you will be able to obtain similar results in your own life.

You may not be able to get someone to commit to mentoring you formally, but you can listen to others who have powerful prayer lives and learn from them. You can observe their lifestyle and learn from their actual prayers. They can also share what scriptures they focus on to support their prayer lives. Another way of tapping into the discipline of prayer is to take courses on prayer or to read good books on the subject.

After following Jesus and seeing his strong relationship with the Father, the disciples asked Christ to teach them how to pray (Luke 11:1). Jesus then taught them how to pray and shared with them the Lord's Prayer as a model for their own prayer lives.
   Your Prayer life is to be constantly developed, as it is your way of communicating with the Creator. Concerning the discipline of prayer, Paul said, "Pray without ceasing," (1 Thessalonians 5:17), which means that you should constantly be in a mode of prayer.

I would add that you need to spend time in prayer and develop a routine prayer life that includes praying to God, writing notes in a journal of what you are learning through prayer, and noting when God answers your prayers. It is important for you to pray consistently and notice what God is doing in your life through prayer. Also, you will notice that God is speaking to you primarily through the word but as you grow in your prayer life, he may begin speaking to you in your spirit as well. It is quite helpful having a system of daily prayer that helps you to constantly stay in communication with God. I often have a "Quiet Time," with God that includes both bible study and prayer.

The Skill of Worship

Much like bible study and prayer, worship is a spiritual skill. You have to spend time worshipping God yourself. You need mature Christian mentors and models; proven and tested that will help you to grow in God, but you must also commit to the practice of worship. Mentors are mature believers who can teach you things about the Christian life. Models are principles that you can learn from bible characters or mature Christians from the past. I prefer to select models from people who are no longer living. The reason for that is you can observe how the principles they upheld worked out in their lives.

In order to grow and flourish as a mature follower

of Jesus, you must learn to cultivate the heart of a worshipper, so that you can mature in the spiritual skill of worship. The way to excel in worship is to experience worship, learn from mentors, model great worshippers from the past, and then repeat the process. When you repeat the process, your worship experience will be informed by your mentor's wisdom and the biblical models you are imitating in your daily life, which leads to a deeper and better understanding of worship.

PART I
WORSHIP EXAMINED

1.

You Were Created to Worship

"Now is, when the true worshippers shall worship the Father in spirit and in truth: for the Father seeketh such to worship him. God is a Spirit: and they that worship him must worship him in spirit and in truth."

John 4:23-24

In the early 1980s my family and I lived in a small town called Cambridge, just west of Toronto, Ontario. We used to rent a small fire hall for our church services on Sundays. The hall was on the top of the fire department building and I remember having to climb the stairs on a weekly basis to enter this undersized space in hopes to have Sunday services. There weren't many people at that church, but I recall that we used to have wonderful sessions of worship. I remember seeing other members of the church experience God in deep and meaningful ways. Those days of divine appointments with God had a significant impact on me.

We regularly practiced [worship] in our corporate gatherings on Sundays [at that lit]tle fire hall. I can still remember the hand[s, the s]miling faces, and shouts of worship from [the score]s of people who really loved God. In thos[e times peo]ple really desired to experience the prese[nce of th]e Lord. I learned through those intense spiritual experiences that worship in a group setting could be such a blessing. During those times we had the opportunity to connect with God through music, and song. In unison, we lifted our voices in praise to the God that we loved and trusted.

In fairness, not every service was filled with worship and joy. At times services were boring and dry. In addition, not every person in the church was excited about worship. Some people lacked passion and a few of them even demonstrated their disinterest during high points in our corporate worship. Those negative individuals at times would say that they didn't enjoy the service. We would then have to remind them that was understandable because we were not worshipping them, we were worshipping God.

Nevertheless, there were a good number of mature believers that were on fire for God and poured out their entire hearts to God during praise and worship at that little Cambridge church. These are the

worshippers that I looked to mentor me when I was young and learning to praise the Lord.

It is helpful in your growth to be aware that there are varying degrees of connection within any given worship service as some people are more connected to God than others. When you see people deeply bonding with God in worship allow them to inspire you to do the same. When you admire a mature believer who possesses deep periods of worship get to know them and ask them questions so that you can learn and grow in your worship encounters. I like being around those who are on fire for God and who can pour out their entire heart to Him.

Another memory from my youth was when I attended choir practice at our headquarters church in Toronto, Canada. We had a choir leader named Elder MacPherson and he was such a kind and gentle spiritual mentor. When we rehearsed, Elder MacPherson spent much time emphasizing that we needed to model our worship after King David in order to tap into the presence of God. He would let us know it was not good enough to have beautiful music and nice voices. We needed to worship like the church worshipped on the day of Pentecost, as the point of worship was to encounter and to enjoy God's presence. He emphasized that if God didn't show up the choir did not fulfill its purpose. Elder

MacPherson wasn't satisfied until God showed up in our worship!

Those lessons of worship from my youth have stayed with me even until today. I am always excited about praising God and believe it or not, a heart of worship is what is needed from God's people. Worship is not just about how you sound or how you look, when worshipping, your focus should be on pleasing the Lord. A by-product of worshipping God is that you can feel His presence and in His presence is fullness of joy (Psalm 16:11). An indicator that you are experiencing God's presence in worship is that it feels like you and God are alone, despite being in a room filled with people. That's how I often felt during worship while growing up in church and that's an indicator that   God was with me!

Worship the Ultimate Concern

This book will be focusing on the benefits of corporate and private worship. It is important to mention that worship is more than just singing songs and enjoying music. Only those who have a relationship with God can truly encounter this life-changing experience. True worship happens when you put God first and acknowledge that the Lord is the source and the sustainer of life. In other words, God is your ultimate concern, and you should love him more than money, popularity, power, pleasure, or anything else.

On one occasion when Jesus was ministering a lawyer asked him, which was the greatest commandment. Jesus said, "Thou shalt love the Lord thy God with all thy heart, and with all thy soul, and with all thy mind" (Matthew 22:37). Simply put God must be your number one priority, the creator must be your ultimate concern.

You Were Created to Worship

Every living being was designed to praise their Creator, and every human being was conceived for the purpose of worshipping God. "This is life eternal, that they might know you the only true God, and Jesus Christ, whom you have sent" (John 17:3). Those that worship are brought into connection with the love of God. Moreover, as you connect to that immense love, not only does God reveal Himself to you, but He causes you to know yourself in a much deeper sense.

You were created to be a worshipper, and one of the benefits of such a life is that the more you worship, is the more you understand God, and the more you understand God is the more you understand yourself. Moreover, the more you understand who you are, the more you understand that you were created to worship. The bible says, "Trust in the Lord with all of your heart, and lean not to your own understanding. In all your ways acknowledge him, and he will direct your paths," (Proverbs 3:5-6).

The primary reason for creation was to worship God. When God created humanity, He did so for His pleasure. One of the ways in which you please God is to worship Him. "O come, let us worship and bow down: let us kneel before the LORD our maker" (Psalm 95:6). Jesus reminds us that, "Now is, when the true worshippers shall worship the Father in spirit and in truth: for the Father seeketh such to worship him. God is a spirit: and they that worship him must worship him in spirit and in truth" (John 4:23-24).

Worship is a universal call to humanity and despite the fact that many do not answer the call it is still one that is within the nature of all people. The psalmist said, "Let everything that hath breath praise the LORD. Praise ye the LORD" (Psalm 150:6). When a person is connected with God worship becomes natural to them. It has often been preached that there is a void in all of us that only God can fill. When a person finds God, the Lord fills that void within them and it becomes second nature to worship, out of thanksgiving for a life transformed by the grace and mercy of the Lord.

2.

What is Worship?

"And above all these things put on charity (love), which is the bond of perfectness. And let the peace of God rule in your hearts, to the which also ye are called in one body; and be ye, thankful. Let the word of Christ dwell in you richly in all wisdom; teaching and admonishing one another in psalms and hymns and spiritual songs, singing with grace in your hearts to the Lord."

Colossians 3:14-16

In the early 1990's I attended a spiritually powerful church in Toronto that emphasized the importance of having a genuine encounter with God. I was taught that it was vitally important to connect with God and to experience His presence in worship. The leaders of the church would often say, "In *God's* presence is fullness of joy; at His right hand are pleasures for evermore" (Psalms 16:11). I experienced that truth on many occasions and it started me on a lifelong journey of both experiencing and trying to understand the spiritual skill of worship.

Praise vs. Worship

The words praise and worship are very similar, and they both describe the activity of focusing your attention on God through adoration, sacrifice, and/or music. The word praise means "the offering of thankful homage in words or song, as an act of worship: a hymn of praise to God." Eerdmans Dictionary defines praise as, "An expression of worship which recognizes and acknowledges God as the ultimate source and giver of all good gifts. There are several words used for praise in the bible many of which describe the physical activity of praise such as lifting your hands, bowing down, etc.

Worship on the other hand in the New Testament is translated as proskuneo which means, "Fall down before" or "bow down before." Eerdmans Dictionary defines worship as, "An appropriate human response to the magnificent glory of God. Jesus describes worship as a state of the spirit and truth. Worship is both an internal attitude of love and an external practice of truth through words and actions.

Many scholars and worship leaders today define worship as a deeper form of praise. As everything (man, beast, birds, insects, and things living in the seas) is expected to praise the Lord (Psalms 150:6). Worship is a deeper form of praise because worship is accomplished by an exclusive group of believers that God chooses as He is seeking true worshippers (John 4:23). Therefore, not everyone can engage in true worship, as genuine worship requires a relationship with God that is growing and vibrant. Nevertheless, everyone has access to praise the Lord if they can focus on God and what he has done for them.

Definition of Worship

There has been much confusion around what worship is. After much searching and personal contemplation, I believe it is best defined as follows. **Worship is your love expressed towards God in reaction to His love expressed towards you.** In addition the more focused we are in worshipping the true God, the deeper the connection we derive in our time of worship. That was why God encouraged his people throughout history to build him an altar (a place in which they could focus on Him). Although there are various forms of worship in the scriptures, in modern day settings, worship oftentimes is expressed through instruments, our bodies (dancing), and our voices.

In all cultures around the world whenever people are celebrating, they turn to music and singing to set an atmosphere of praise towards the object of their excitement. At sporting events, music is played loudly and people enjoy the performance of their teams hoping for victory and electrifying entertainment. In celebrations like birthdays, weddings, baby showers, festivals, and work office parties music accompanies the merriment. Therefore, if you are excited about God, it is natural to show thanks through music and celebration.

Why Should You Worship God?

What is the purpose of worship and why should you worship God? That sounds like a simple question and in fairness, there are billions of reasons why we should worship God. In reviewing the definition of worship, it is clear that you should worship because you owe it to God for the love that He has given to you. It is 100% true that you should worship God because He is worthy, but God makes it clear that you should also worship Him because of your love for Him.

Nevertheless, there are countless other reasons why you should praise the Lord. As mentioned earlier, you should worship God because of who He is; the Lord is worthy of your obedience and thanksgiving. You should praise God because you were created to praise Him. "Let everything that has breath praise the Lord. Praise ye the LORD," (Psalm 150:6). You should praise God because you love Him.

Furthermore, there are numerous blessings associated with worshipping God. You should praise the Lord because of the blessings and benefits of worshipping God. We will be covering several of such benefits in this book.

What is your top 10 list of benefits related to worshipping God? If you want to forward your list to us, we would love to hear from you at www.nevillesolomon.com.

General Worship Vs Focused Worship

There are various ways that you can worship God in your life. I have put worship into two major categories namely general worship and focused worship. You can worship God through your employment, you can worship God by caring for your family members, and you can worship God by giving to the poor. You can spend time laughing with friends, encouraging your neighbor, working in a soup kitchen, and/or sitting in silence and meditating. All these actions can be defined as sincere times of worship. There are many ways that you can worship the Lord.

From a theological perspective whatever you do in

word or deed, you should do it all in the name of Jesus (Colossians 3:17). So going to work is a deep form of devotion to God especially if you honor the Lord in your tithes and offerings. Feeding your children is a deep form of devotion to the Lord especially if you dedicate your children to God. Evangelism is a central work of the church and when you share the gospel with others that is a practice of deep devotion to God because unbelievers' lives are being impacted by the good news of God. However, I define these good deeds as general worship. That means that although they demonstrate your dedication to God these deeds do not demand that you give 100% of our attention to God.

General worship is an attempt at multitasking between two or more things on the one hand and God on the other. Not all of your energy is centred on God. When you worship within the category of general worship. You pay attention to something else while trying to worship God, which results in you not being fully engaged in the process of praise and worship.

When you attempt to honour God through your work, it amounts to a good gesture, but the true purpose of work is not to worship. The true purpose of work is to make money and to fulfill the agenda of your workplace. That means 100% of your focus can't be on God when you are at work. If all your focus is on God when you are working, then that means that you are unfaithful in your commitment to your place of employment.

Even if you are in full-time ministry serving God, your focus is not fully on praising the Lord because much of your effort is on ministering to people. Although much of your activity in ministry is motivated to serve the Lord, however, 100% of your focus isn't on worshipping God even if you are ministering to people in the church. That is why serving God through your work or your ministry is categorized as general worship.

Focused worship on the other hand is the exact opposite of general worship. Focused worship is when a person sets aside time to focus 100% on worshipping God without distractions. These times of focused worship usually take place in corporate or private worship. Corporate worship typically happens at church with other believers, and private worship primarily takes place at home when you are alone or in a small group setting. These are times when there is an opportunity to pay full attention to the Lord.

Focused worship is commonly associated with singing and music. In certain cultures, dancing and other artistic expressions are utilized as well. For most Christians, the corporate Sunday morning service is the place that they commonly have focused worship. That means that you can put all of your attention on God, and engage in the spiritual exercises of lifting up the name of Jesus Christ.

At most Sunday church celebrations, music is usually played, and singing is expected not only from those on the platform but from all who attend the service. Songs that are sung are designed to touch God's heart. During these periods of focused worship, the church has a shared experience of touching God and giving Him their undivided attention.

Focused worship can also take place in your home in a small group or when you are by yourself. A home is an excellent place to praise the Lord and to set aside time to concentrate 100% on God. You can worship the Lord through singing, prayer, and quiet contemplation in a small group, as a family, or just by yourself. Music can be used in these worship experiences, but you can also sing acapella.

Worship Is a Mentality

The bible is filled with countless examples of worshippers and King David proves to be the best model of such a worshipper. David would dance, sing, play music, celebrate and make the Lord his ultimate priority. The bible says that David was a man after God's own heart (Acts 13:22). The goal of every worshipper should be to make God number one in his/her life.

Worship is a mentality of gratitude, respect, and love towards God. (Romans 12:2) tells you "Not to conform to this world: but to be transformed by the renewing of your mind, that you may prove what is that good, and acceptable, and perfect will of God. When you worship, you have to worship with a renewed and transformed mind recognizing what's good about God. The typical worldly mindset views God in a negative way. Nevertheless, the pure in heart celebrate God for His goodness and His mercy.

Worship is a lifestyle and you should have a mentality of thanksgiving towards the Lord. I have trained myself to have periods of focused worship in which I remember God's forgiveness and His love. Worship has always been significant to me. Like David, I enjoyed singing, composing music, and expressing myself through the arts, in praise of God. I love dancing during praises but must admit that dancing is definitely not my gift.

I could spend hours detailing why God is good. The more you are able to inform yourself with the truths of the Word, the more you will empower yourself to worship the Lord. God is faithful, honest, just, kind, merciful, righteous, holy, creative, and loving. If you study the Word from Genesis to Revelation and focus on the character of God; you will have enough fuel to worship God forever.

"For I know the thoughts that I think toward you, saith the LORD, thoughts of peace, and not of evil, to give you an expected end," (Jeremiah 29:11). Focused worship is fueled by what you know about God. "There is therefore, no condemnation to them which are in Christ Jesus, who walk not after the flesh, but after the Spirit," (Romans 8:1). Focus on God's goodness and grow in your relationship with Him.

3.

5 Benefits of Worship

"Bless the LORD, O my soul, and forget not all his benefits:" Psalm 103:2

There are many benefits to having a focused worship experience with God. When you give 100% of your attention to God, it transforms you. So many people in life don't know who God is, but the worshipper is provided with the opportunity to know God in an intimate manner. The more time you spend with God in worship the more you will grow in the spiritual skill of worship.

You may wonder where I got this idea of the five major benefits of worship. Firstly, I must confess that there are far more than 5 benefits of worshipping God. But the five major benefits became apparent to me through intense study of the word, godly mentors, and the practical application of observed facts from biblical models.

Ultimately the Holy Spirit revealed to me through my own spiritual development these 5 major benefits that I will be sharing with you. Furthermore, I am an extremist when it comes to worshipping God and the constant time in worship has opened up my eyes to the spiritual skill of praise and worship. My dedication to worshipping God has unlocked the secret of these five life-changing benefits. Before disclosing more about my worship experience, I wanted to share four foundational keys to receiving the benefits of worship.

Firstly, we are all called to worship God and Him alone. Most definitely, God needs to be first in our lives. He must be the ultimate priority. That means you have no other gods, before Him (Exodus 20:3). Some people desire to be Christians and they hold unto other gods for their security and comfort.

These false gods may come in the forms of physical idols like statues, paintings and ancient land marks or temples. These misguided worshippers may serve false deities like Baal, and Zeus, or in modern times, they may put their ultimate faith in good luck charms, human relationships, materialism, money, or in a false philosophical belief about the actual nature of the true God.

As mentioned early we should put nothing before the Lord as God must be the first and only God in our life.

If you have any other gods, you will more than likely have little or no access to the five benefits of worship.

Secondly, you are all called to follow and serve God. The scripture declares, "For as many as are led by the Spirit of God, they are the sons of God," (Romans 8:14). Those who are true worshippers are those who are led by the Holy Spirit. If you are led by the Holy Spirit, you will obey God's Word and will serve Him. Many nonbelievers would like to enjoy the 5 benefits of worship, but if they don't have a genuine relationship with God, they will more than likely have little or no access to the five benefits of worship.

Thirdly, you are all called to war against the purpose and the will of the devil. Jesus was victorious on the cross and true worship is grounded in that truth. Since you are free from sin and the grip of the devil, you are called to celebrate Christ and to resist the devil until he flees from you (James 4:7). There is a conflict in this world between the kingdom of darkness and the kingdom of light and you must make a conscious decision to be on the side of light. If you are a committed worshipper then that means you are about spreading the gospel of the kingdom of God also known as the kingdom of light. That means when the devil and evil situations attack, you fight back through trusting the Lord and believing the promises of His Word. If you don't trust the Lord and employ your faith to oppose evil you will more than likely have little or no access to the five benefits of worship.

Lastly, worship is always the result of a revelation; God has to teach you how to worship. The blessing of worship is that God actually becomes your mentor and teaches you directly how to worship in spirit and in truth. You need to have an authentic experience with God or at minimum, desire such an experience prior to obtaining and recognizing the five benefits of worship in your life. Worship is never the result of human initiative. It is not like investing money in the bank, where you give God worship and He is obligated to give you benefits. Worship is a relationship with God and you receive His benefits because you are His child and He chooses to bless you. So, without a revelation of God, you will more than likely have little or no access to the five benefits of worship.

In some rare cases when God blesses those who don't put Him first, who don't serve Him, who don't war against the devil, and those who don't have a revelation of who He is; sadly, those individuals don't recognize the blessings and frequently attribute God's kindness to luck or coincidence. This is because unbelievers are often blind to God's blessings and miracles.

In the case that you have a relationship with God, and you are being led by the Holy Spirit, you fight against the devil and you have a growing revelation of who God is, then you have the opportunity to tap into the five benefits of worship.

I promised to disclose more about my worship experience and how I came across the five major benefits of worship. It all started in my mother's basement when I was about twenty years old. I was severely down in my spirit and couldn't figure out what the issue was. For the most part, my life was going pretty well. I had an amazing family, I had great friends, and I was doing everything in life that I wanted to do. I couldn't figure out what was wrong as everything appeared to be good from my perspective.

I heard a lot about clinical depression and I believe that to be a real and serious issue for many people but I had a strong feeling that wasn't my issue; as I was a relatively happy person throughout my life and never had an issue like this before. Nevertheless, despite being emotionally down I felt that this issue had a spiritual root.

You see I was attending York University in the city of Toronto, and concentrated all of my attention on my studies while neglecting my worship time with

God. At first, things were good, I would hang out with friends have fun, and think to myself that I will attend church more regularly and increase my focused worship in a year or two when I had time. After all, I was too busy to attend to my spiritual life right now as I was pursuing my education. I had a strong view that general worship was just as good as focused worship, as I was serving God by getting good marks at school and God knew my heart.

But after some time, I started to notice a change for the worse. At first, I thought it was the stress of school, but after going through that experience, one day while in my mom's basement, I realized that the problem wasn't primarily an issue of mental health or even stress, it was actually because my worship life was declining.

On that day in the basement, I came to the conclusion that I was missing a worship relationship with God. For several months I neglected building the spiritual skill of worship in my life, because I wasn't worshipping God, I felt something was missing. The first thing I tried to do was study my bible more regularly and pray, but I felt like something was still not right. So, then I tried listening to worship music and attending church more regularly and even though this helped somewhat I still felt like something was absent.

It wasn't until I gave my life over to the development of the skill of worship and learned how to worship God more effectively with my whole heart that this spiritual depression went away for good. I must make a distinction here as it relates to clinical depression and spiritual growth. If a person has a mental health problems and requires medications, more than likely, improvement in the level of the spiritual skill of worship will not solve their situation.

I believe that God can and does work miracles, but you should take your medications as you wait for your miracle. When saints have high blood pressure, they continue to take their medications because they know the possible consequences of not caring for their illness. The same is true to mental health God provided the wisdom and the science behind mental health and medication. Therefore if we respect God we should respect what the Lord is doing as it relates to the developments within our health system.

When I speak about my situation when I started to worship God the spiritual oppression lifted. Some issues in our are spiritual in nature and for that reason require a spiritual solution. That is why I feel that worship is a critical discipline that all Christians need to grow in, to overcome the power of the enemy.

After this transformation and victory over the enemy,

I started to realize that there were some major benefits to worshipping God. I had always been aware that worship helped me to build a stronger relationship with the Lord, but after this experience, I started to come into the revelation that the worshipper had access to other miraculous benefits. As I grew in the spiritual skill of worship, I studied the Word, prayed, and God started to reveal to me the five benefits of worship.

In life there are so many challenges designed to separate you from God; the devil, the world, and the cares of life work together to oppose your worship. When I realized my issue wasn't medical but spiritual and that the reason, I felt emptiness within was a result of being immature in my worship. My goal was to prioritize spending time in worship with God.

It's a funny thing because if you practice neglecting worship over time, it feels normal. You will get bored during times of worship and would want to sleep, because you are immature in this spiritual skill. When you are used to being in a state of worship it becomes normal to you, and you will be excited, alert, and happy when you have opportunity to worship. Despite this truth, you still need to guard your heart to ensure that your worship life doesn't lead to you not appreciating the special opportunity of worshipping the Lord on a regular basis.

If you find you're disinterested in worship, or if you find you're not appreciating your time with God as you did in the past. It's time to focus on developing the skill of worship in your life. If you find yourself depressed and spiritually down like me when I was in my mom's basement don't give up. Your worship is under attack!

Now is the time to develop the skill of worship by spending focused time with God alone or in a group setting, and putting 100% of your focus on God. Worship needs to be a major part of your life once again. For those of you who are doing well and have regular powerful periods of worship with God, you need to lift your worship to an even higher level and ask God to move in your life like never before.

Over the years I have heard people say that in today's world people don't praise God the way our father's used to. When I started to get serious about worshipping God, I discovered that in order for that statement to be true I would have to include myself in it. But if I could commit my life to worshipping God, then I could experience God in the phenomenon therefore, making that claim a false statement. One of the reasons why I have written this book is to inspire a generation to believe in God for transformative worship.

God has shown me that worship is about intimacy and the closer I get to God, the more God sets me free from the things that try to bind me. I am free from the chains of doubt and unbelief through the power of praise and worship. Praise and worship have set me free from fear and doubt. Praise and worship can set you free from all fear and doubts. Praise and worship can bring you into the path of God's blessings. I believe that the spiritual skill of worship is a foundational requirement for knowing God is a deep and more meaningful way.

I recall that day in the basement when I was sadden in my spirit, it was a blessing in some way because I started to value the power of worship like never before. When you compare life in fellowship with the Holy Spirit, and life separated from the Holy Spirit, you realize that the two are drastically different ways of living. One of the great problems in life is that you can't tell what you are missing in worship until you are aware of what it feels like to connect with God. When you don't have access to the benefits of worship, the natural response is a lack of interest in God, that we manifest through boredom, confusion, or even depression. When you have access to the benefits of worship and you are aware of what God is doing in your life, the natural reaction is joy.

Once I realized that worship was the key to my life

being transformed by Christ and that the knowledge of the benefits of worship was the key to staying motivated in worship, that's when I became more passionate about worship and my spiritual growth started to advance tremendously. Many of the great worshippers that I know are so filled with joy and wisdom. If you discover that worship is a weak area in your life or you want to improve your connection with God; be confident that when you understand the five benefits of worship you will be more sensitive to the things of the spirit and the value of worship itself.

When engaging in authentic worship, the worshipper is blessed with numerous benefits. **The following are the five major benefits of focused worship...**

1. **Worship is a Fragrance**
2. **Worship is a Teacher**
3. **Worship is a Weapon**
4. **Worship is Medicine**
5. **Worship is a Family Business**

I didn't discover the five benefits of worship immediately and I didn't discover them all at one time, but owing to the several years spent in personal worship, God revealed to me five ways that He invests in worshippers.

Worship is a fragrance and just as God enjoys the sweet smell of our worship; the authentic worshipper is connected to God through the act of genuine praise. This is the greatest benefit of worship, which is to be connected to God. When I speak of worship as a fragrance, I am talking about how God connects with you through worship.

Worship is a teacher, worship is primarily you communicating with God; however, He will speak back to you in worship. He will open up the scriptures and help you to have an in-depth understanding of the Word when you praise Him. God will convict you in your heart and teach you things like how to forgive your neighbor, how to better understand the love of God, how to invest your life, and many more things. When I speak of worship as a teacher, I am talking about how God leads and guides you when you worship Him.

I learned that worship is a weapon and have seen proof of this through the scriptures and also in my own personal experiences. When I needed help in my life I would go into praising God and at times almost immediately God would answer my need. Even in those times when my needs were not answered right away, I could see God's hand moving. I felt protected and more at peace due to the power of worship. When I speak of worship as a weapon,

I am talking about how God protects you from dangers seen and unseen.

I learned that worship is medicine. This is not only true for physical illnesses, but even more so, for injuries within your soul. God is able to heal past hurts and pains. He is able to heal childhood trauma and abuse. In the midst of worshipping, when you feel like giving up all of a sudden joy can cover you, and liberate you. When I speak of worship as medicine, I am talking about how God can heal you, body, soul, and spirit.

Lastly, I learned that worship is a family business. God's business is not one of dollars and cents but the saving of souls and the transformation of lives. God awakens spiritual gifts within you when you worship so that you can accomplish His will on the earth and serve Him. God gives you spiritual gifts, and you can also discover and operate in these gifts by worshipping, as worship often activates your spiritual gifts and your purpose. When I speak of worship as a family business, I am talking about how God can reveal to you His will for your life.

PART II
5 BENEFITS OF WORSHIP

4.

Worship is a Fragrance

"For we are unto God a sweet savor of Christ, in them that are saved." 2 Corinthians 2:15

If you are a follower of God, you should produce a fragrance of worship that God recognizes. For that reason, worship is not a sound, it's not a voice, it's not a song, but it is a fragrance. When speaking about worship being a fragrance, what I mean is that worship has the ability to connect you to God. When you offer God your praise the Lord has the choice to accept or reject it. When Cain and Able offered sacrifices of praise to God the Lord accepted Abel's worship and rejected Cain's (Genesis 4:3-6).

Why was that? Why did God accept Abel's sacrifice and rejected Cain's? It's because God knows the motives of your heart. When you give God your best it creates a fragrance that is pleasing to Him. If you offer God something that you don't respect, it produces a horrible odor in His nostrils. The worshipper should be far more concerned about God accepting his/her praise, than whether the music or their voice sounds good.

However, those who lead worship at church often spend much of their energy trying to create excellence through rehearsal as it relates to the quality of the music and the voices. Very little time is spent to ensure that the fragrance of their worship smells delightful. However, the true goal of worship should be to cultivate a relationship with God and to inspire those in worship to cultivate a fragrance in worship that ushers in the presence of God. You can only truly have a connection with God in worship if you have a profound appreciation and devotion towards Him.

You may have a deep longing to be connected to God and to feel His presence, but until you learn to emit a fragrance of thanksgiving you will struggle in connecting with the Lord. Many worshippers testify that when they worship, they can feel the power of the Holy Spirit moving in their lives. During this time of focused worship, they have been able to connect with God by loving and thanking Him through the worship experience.

In the book of Exodus God requested that Pharaoh permit His people to worship Him. The Lord had heard the cry of the children of Israel and smelt the pain of their slavery under the oppression of Egypt (Exodus 3:9). God then said to Pharaoh, "Let my People Go." He was so serious about connecting with His people through focused worship that the Lord freed them with numerous miracles from the bondage of Egypt.

In the New Testament, the disciple John advised that Jesus told the Samaritan woman that God is seeking worshippers that will worship the Lord in "Spirit and in Truth," (John 4:23-24). God is looking to connect with you, not just on a fleshly level. The Lord wants His Spirit to connect with your spirit so that you can be in a relationship with Him. If you draw near to God the Lord promises that He will draw near to you (James 4:8). Worship is one of the primary ways that we are connected to the Creator. When you worship, it produces a fragrance that is pleasing to God and this sweet savor connects you to His presence. Worship is ultimately about providing God with a gift of love that is acceptable.

For example, Esther spent a whole year in preparation to meet her future husband, who was also the king of Persia. She was anointed with scented oils every day so that when she was presented before the king she could be chosen as his bride (See Esther 2:12). I believe that an aspect of worship as a fragrance that could be missed was that

Esther spent 12 months applying oils and perfumes so that she would be pleasing to her royal companion. For that same reason, the worship of the believer needs to be anointed so that when the King of Kings encounters your worship it will be well-pleasing to Him.

You need to consistently express your praise and worship to the Lord until it produces a spiritual fragrance that moves the Creator to respond. You should not provide God with what you have leftover. A take it or leave it praise. You should be like Esther and provide God with your best. As true praise produces a sweet smelling fragrance that pleases the nostrils of God and blesses the thankful worshipper.

Worship as I mentioned earlier is like a gym and you need to exercise your praise regularly so that during times of worship you can celebrate God and produce a sweet-smelling praise. If you fail to produce such a fragrance you will find your praise to be in the category of Cain's praise, which was rejected by God. You don't want to give God dead praise because there is no power in dead praises. True praise invokes the presence of God.

5.

Worship is a Teacher

"The anointing which you have received of the Lord abides in you and teaches you all things, and is the truth." 1 John 2:27

True worship leads you to recognize and identify God as a teacher. According to John, the anointing which you have received of the Lord abides in you and teaches you all things, and is the truth (1 John 2:27). In times of worship, the voice of God can become clearer and you can build a powerful relationship with the Lord. Moreover, the Oxford Dictionary defines the term "teach" as "to show or explain to someone how to do something." Webster's Dictionary defines the term as "means to cause to acquire knowledge or skill; it applies to any manner of imparting information or skill so that others may learn."

Since God is all-knowing and all-powerful that means that you can learn all things from Him. Therefore, worship is an experience that can open up your awareness to understand things through the Holy Spirit which previously, you may have been unable to understand. In the midst of the worship experience, God can open your understanding to the scriptures, your understanding of your environment, and your understanding of significant problems in your life. By spending time in the Lord's presence, the Holy Spirit can teach you. Awareness is a key benefit when worshipping God, as he can open your eyes to situations that are hidden. Education outside of God builds upon what you already know, but when God teaches you something He can teach you things that you had no frame of reference about.

One of the primary things that God teaches you, is about who He is. Most Christian groups have some formal training in their church about who God is and what he has done in the bible, but a worshipper has an ongoing experience with God that enlightens their understanding of who God is. For example, when you have been forgiven of many sins by the Lord, your awareness is opened to the fact that God is merciful. If you are in need of help and you pray and God provides your needs, your awareness is opened to the fact that the Lord is a provider. Worship expands your awareness to holistically comprehending who God is.

When I speak of awareness in worship, I am speaking about having encounters with God in which the Holy Spirit teaches you knew things. The worshipper expresses their love and appreciation to God and the Lord, in turn, communicates His will and His purpose to them. Worship is much like prayer; in that you talk to God and the Lord is able to talk to you. The more you worship God and are conscious that the Lord is a teacher, the more aware you become of your surroundings. In other words, God will expand your knowledge in relation to your spiritual growth and development in worship.

The Lord has an extreme devotion towards His people. Jesus Christ was sent to the world and gave His life for us. For God so loved the world that He gave his only begotten son, that whosoever believes in him shall not perish, but have everlasting life (John 3:16). The more you understand how much God loves you the more motivated you will be to worship God with a joyful heart (See Psalms 100). Worship brings your mind to the awareness that God loves you specifically and you can experience that love right now if you connect with God the teacher, in worship. Those who feel that God is not for them or that God doesn't love them have not mastered the skill of connecting with God the teacher and therefore their awareness of his kindness is limited.

God loves you and hears you He also helps you to be able to hear His voice. God teaches you to come into a relationship with Him and in that relationship,

He teaches you how-to walk-in dominion and to live out the truth of His words. The worship experience can be a time in which God can train you and open your awareness to these facts. You have to learn how to tap into God as your teacher. For those gifted in worship, many have learned that God can talk to them about their gifts, about major life decisions, and much more. At times the Lord will even speak to you about secret things that He is doing in the world and reveal things to you that could change your life and the life of those around you.

I have personally been in worship and on countless occasions, God has brought back a scripture to mind that really helped me with a difficult decision. As it relates to my ministry as a preacher God, has opened my awareness in the midst of worship about what I should preach, He has spoken to me about changes I needed to make in my business and changes I needed to make as it related to my personal health.

God can teach you anything during worship, and in the midst of focused worship, you can hear His voice clearly. For some people, this is hard to believe that God can talk to you. That is why I emphasized having focused worship is essential. Spending such attentive times with God allows you to discover things about God that you were unaware of. Much like Elisha's servant who looked out and saw that the enemies of Elisha the prophet outnumbered them, Elisha then prayed for God to open the servant's eyes, and the servant looked out and saw the hills full of God's supernatural army (2Kings 6:17).

God's unseen army was far greater in power and size than the enemies that Elisha's servant could see. Supernatural awareness can come by listening to the Spirit of God when He speaks. Under normal circumstances, you cannot see what God is doing behind the scenes but if you worship and listen to the Holy Spirit, the Lord can teach you things about the supernatural realm that you are unaware of.

Most times God will teach you the truths of life by opening your understanding of the scriptures. The awareness you obtain in worship opens up the Word of God so that you can understand it better and know the proper way to apply the Word in practical ways.

The Lord can also teach you how to manage your inner world during times of worship. God can show you how to be happy no matter what you are going through. In *God's* presence is fullness of joy; at *God's* right hand are pleasures for evermore (Psalm 16:11). The greater your awareness of who God is and the power of His Word, the happier you will be. God is able to teach you the path to true happiness and fulfillment when you draw closer to Him and open your ears to learn His truths.

God can teach you anything and if you are willing to go on that journey with Him the Lord will teach you the art of happiness. Simply put, the skill of happiness is living your life by God's design. It is the ability to submit to God's will and live your life the way the Lord intends. God is a teacher and will teach you through worship about every area in your life. God can open your awareness if you worship Him with passion and are willing to be teachable.

6.

Worship is a Weapon

"For the weapons of our warfare are not carnal, but mighty through God to the pulling down of strong holds;" 2 Corinthians 10:4

Christians often speak fearfully when talking about the devil and his power on the earth. Some say, "Don't you know that Satan is the god of this world," (2 Corinthians 4:4). But these same people forget that the Lord Almighty is the God of Satan. Satan is a small **god.** The divine creator you serve is the big **GOD** who has dominion and authority over everything including the devil. The great and powerful God of the universe cares for you and your wellbeing. He will protect you from Satan, and one of the major ways that He will protect you is through the power of worship.

God has given you a weapon that the devil and his cohorts of darkness cannot compete against and that weapon is worship. Worship is a powerful force that can stand against the enemy and his attacks against you. If you know how to use this divine weapon you will do massive damage to the kingdom of darkness. God has created you to walk in victory and to possess dominion on the earth. You should not allow darkness to control any area of your life, because you belong to God and you are free by the blood of Jesus Christ.

When Israel was going to war with their enemies under the rule of King Jehoshaphat, he appointed men to sing and praise God and to stand at the front of the army. They played instruments, sang songs, and worship God intensely as they marched forward to battle. The army was victorious without having to physically fight the battle as God fought their battle for them (2 Chronicles 20:15). When you worship and praise God you wage war against all the plans of the devil. Worship draws you into the presence of God and God's presence destroys the authority and the plans of the enemy.

It is important to mention that the most powerful aspect of worship as it relates to warfare is that worship associates you with Jesus Christ. Christ's benefits and His power are imputed to you by the power of association. You are associated with God through your faith in Jesus. Therefore, you are not warring against the enemy by the direct actions of your worship. Your worship connects you to Jesus and He wars with the enemy on your behalf.

An example of the power of association in the Old Testament was when God called Abraham to the promised land. God never called Lot but Lot was extremely blessed because he was associated with Abraham. Lot was blessed by God with all the blessings of Abraham. A great name, strength, riches, a fine family, a huge network of associates and staff were granted to Lot because he was connected to Abraham. When Lot separated himself from Abraham; the source of his blessings, and went off on his own, Lot eventually lost everything (See Genesis 19). We are like Lot in many ways in the sense that all of our blessings come from Jesus and without Christ, we can do nothing. This is directly related to spiritual warfare as you obtain victory over the enemy by the power of God, and not by your own might.

In the New Testament, Paul and Silas were jailed for sharing the gospel. They were in jail with no way to escape. But at midnight when they began to worship God, there was an earthquake and the prison doors were open (Acts 16:24-26). It doesn't matter what tries to enslave you, when you are in association with Jesus Christ through worship you will be set free. Praise and worship can open doors that are shut, and deliver you from bondage.

If you feel unhappy or overwhelmed you should worship God. Lifting up the name of Jesus is a spiritual weapon that can liberate you from the bondage of your flesh. If you give your issue over to Christ, you invite the Lord who has no limits to address that problem with all the power of heaven. It's not your might that solves your problems, but your association with the mighty God that solves your problems.

Worship is immensely powerful and it can deliver you from demonic oppression. The bible tells us when King Saul was tormented by an evil spirit (I Samuel 16:14) that David who was anointed in worship played the harp for Saul and this provided deliverance for the spiritually oppressed King Saul (I Samuel 16:23). David was blessed by God and because Saul was in association with a man blessed by God, he received the blessings of the young shepherd boy.

But the question comes where did David get his blessings from and where did Abraham get his blessings from. The answer is that they were in association with God and everything they received was because they were in a relationship with the Lord through worship. The key to victory in life is to be connected with the creator in worship.

I recall when I went to India in 2010 with a team of Ministers, we entered a little house with a few local church members. It was late that night as I preached in a remote village ministering to the people. We joined together in praising God and all of a sudden something strange happened. In the middle of the worship service, a local village girl who was demon-possessed came to the door and started banging on the door. She was screaming to us stop tormenting me! It was a demon speaking through her and the worship that we were giving to God was a weapon tormenting the evil spirit within that young girl.

We then opened the door and addressed this demon-possessed young lady. We continued to worship God and prayed for this young girl and in less than 5 minutes she was delivered from those demons and we all praised God in thanksgiving. The act of powerful worship tortured those demons that possessed her. In that moment of intimacy with God, we were able to rebuke that evil spirit and see it flee. The demons didn't flee because we had great music or were singing in tune. The evil spirits left the girl because we employed worship as a weapon and through faith commanded them to go. They took flight and ran away because we were in association with a righteous God who showed up in that village and touched that young woman.

When I speak of worship being a weapon the concept is threefold. Firstly, worship protects you from the attacks of the enemy. No weapon that is formed against you shall prosper, and every tongue that shall rise against you in judgment, you shall condemn (Isaiah 54:17). The enemy might come after you and may even try to harm you but when you are a worshipper God will defend you. When the enemy shall come in like a flood, the Spirit of the Lord shall lift up a standard against him.

Secondly, God will attack what is attacking you. When Daniel was betrayed and thrown into the lion's den because of the schemes of his peers God delivered Daniel and those who set up to kill him were killed by the same lions by which they intended to harm Daniel (see Daniel chapter 6). When there are traps set up to harm you when you enter into worship God will turn the situation around and the Lord will attack what is trying to attack you.

Thirdly, God will fight on your behalf and bless you when your enemy's intent on harming you. Joseph's brothers sold him into slavery and tried to destroy his future but the hand of the Lord was upon Joseph's life. His brothers sold him into slavery and thought he would have been dead but God protected Joseph's life because he was a worshipper. Joseph said to his brother, "But as for you, you thought evil against me; but God meant it unto the good, to bring to pass, as it is this day to save many people alive," (Genesis 50:20). In other words, enemies plan to harm you but God plans to bless you in the midst of their hatred towards you.

Worship is a weapon and if you will trust in the Lord, He will fight your battles. "Who is the King of glory? The Lord strong and mighty, the LORD mighty in battle," (Psalm 24:8). It is this powerful God who permits you to have victory simply because you worship Him and allow Him to devastate your enemies. God is a warrior and will exact force upon those who oppose His will for your life.

7.

Worship is a Medicine

He says, "I am the Lord that Heals," Exodus 15:26

A promise that God made to ancient Israel and He makes to His church today is that the Lord is a Healer. God is a healer and there is no place that this fact is more evident than when you worship Him. God is the Healer, and worship is the medicine that transforms the physical, psychological, and spiritual health of the believer. You are not working to be healed, as healing is not found in your efforts it is found through God's grace. You should open your heart to receive the healing waters of God's love when you connect with Him through focused worship.

It is important to mention that God does heal outside of the worship experience, but the believer should never overlook the blessings of worship in relation to healing. When you pay attention to God and express your love to Him regularly in focused worship, God can and does heal your body, your soul, and your spirit. So many people have testified to the fact that in the midst of a worship service they or someone they know has been healed instantaneously through the divine medicine of God's love.

There are countless Christians today who ascribe to a belief that God doesn't heal anymore. But if you look at their daily worship experiences it appears like those individuals and churches don't worship God with passion anymore either. They may open their hymnal and have long sad looks on their faces, but they don't connect with their Healer in worship. Healing happens naturally in a healthy vibrant worshipping environment. When you feel the presence of God in worship, you and those around you tend to experience the healing power of God. Many times worshippers experience the hand of God and explain that it feels like a warm heat or goosebumps.

I am aware of numerous people who have experienced the healing power of God. In fairness, not everyone who worships gets physically healed. But there are a great number of people who connect with God, and do experience physical, emotional, and spiritual healing, and for that reason, I believe worship is medicine.

Nonetheless, there are some who would disregard the belief that you can be healed by God as they find the fact that some are not healed as a sign that there is no healing happening in worship. However, you would never assign this logic to hospitals. If only a few people got healed in a hospital you wouldn't say the hospital was fake and was not real. In fact, if anything you would try to figure out how the hospital could develop their systems so that more people could be healed by their institution.

The world has experienced the crisis of covid 19 and despite the hospitals being challenged to handle this virus we celebrate the efforts of doctors and nurses. Even when the hospital staff report that they are losing the battle with the virus we celebrate hospital staff and try to encourage them to do their best.

On the other hand, when speaking about the church if only 90% of the people are healed in a worship service the majority of people would conclude that healings are fake and don't work at all. The one thing we forget many times as believers is that we are all going to die at some point and most of us will enter into heaven due to sickness. Therefore, you are not always going to be healed because you are not going to live forever. Nevertheless, because God is a miracle worker you should tap into the option of healing when it is available and it is often made available through worship.

God is still healing people physically through the worship experience. However, I believe that more people today need inner healing than physical healing. We are living in a world that is filled with stress and turmoil. Mental health is a key issue that needs to be addressed, and taken seriously. I believe that some of the afflictions in your soul is based on spiritual forces that are working against the will of God for your life. In such a case, engaging in worship becomes medicine that can heal from the stress and heaviness of life. Inner healing is a real experience that can happen in the life of the believer as God can work a miracle on the inside of our hearts and minds.

A specific internal healing that needs to be centred on is emotional healing. The older I get the more I appreciate the emotional healings that happen in worship. Countless people today suffer from depression, confusion, lack of motivation, grief, guilt, anger, hatred, lust, and despair. When you experience emotional healing and the peace of God all of these social and psychological ailments come under God's control. The peace of God brings calmness to the life of the worshipper and as you consume your divine medicine the virus of your sinful nature is subjected to the authority of God's Spirit.

Those who are against miracles, often miss God's healing power that is available in none miraculous forms. Many believers from all denominations lack discipline and are overweight and out of shape. One of the primary ways that God can heal you is to direct you to change your lifestyle. You are to eat well, exercise, think pure thoughts, and commune with God and this is the primary means of health for the believer. Many worshippers miss out on this benefit of God's healing.

The worship experience is also able to cleanse you of your sins and purify you through God's power. The ancient songwriter said, "Have mercy upon me, O LORD; for I am weak: O LORD heal me; for my bones are vexed," (Psalm 6:2). David looked to God to heal him of his brokenness when he said, "Have mercy upon me, O God, according to your lovingkindness; according unto the multitude of your tender mercies blot out my transgressions. Wash me thoroughly from my iniquity; and cleanse me from my sin," (Psalm 51:1-2). God's healing power can extend to your spirit and if you repent and believe he can heal you of your sins.

Worship is medicine and if you spend time expressing your love to God you can apply His healing power to your life. The healing capacity of God can be applied to your body, soul, and spirit. God is the doctor not only of your physical health but he can provide inner healing and can forgive you of your sins.

8.

Worship is a Family Business

He said, "... I must be about my Father's business,"
Luke 2:49 (b)

Worship is a family business and God calls His children to work with Him to build His Empire. One of the ways that God builds His Kingdom is to get you to do what you were born to do and that is to operate in your spiritual gifts and your purpose. You were created to lift the name of the Lord up and it is also natural or should I say supernatural for you to worship and work in God's business.

Many times, during and after worship, God performs miracles. He responds to your prayers, provides answers to difficult questions, gives you the power to forgive, exposes your faults so that you can change, warns you, encourages you, and comforts you. But worship is not just about your self-interests there is an aspect of worship that is designed for you to serve God and by extension to serve others. True worship is not selfish in nature. True worship says; not my will but thy will be done (Luke 22:42).

Worship Activates Your Spiritual Gifts

During the worship period, God can activate your spiritual gifts to work for His purpose. I am a teacher and love to teach others the Word of God. At times when I am in worship, God will begin to teach me scriptures in such a way that I get filled with extreme joy. Later when I share these words with others their lives are transformed by my teaching gift.

Worship intensifies your spiritual gifts, and if you are in genuine fellowship with the presence of God, this supernatural event of praise can help to train you and prepare you to better operate in your spiritual gifts. For example, those who sing, worship, dance or create songs, during the worship experience often notice how they grow in their gifting as they engage the Holy Spirit. When you feel the intensified presence of God as a worshipper, it motivates you to express your love towards God even more. Those having the gifts of worship help to build God's spiritual business by inspiring others to worship God in corporate worship and focused worship at home.

Spiritual gifts like preaching, intercessory prayer, and faith can be activated and grown while having focused worship with the Lord. The Lord awakens your gifts so that you will use them for His glory. Some gifts being enhanced in worship are easier to see than others. For example, people who have the gift of giving, desire to give more to their church and can often create plans during the worship experience of how they are going to give back to the community, build a business, help others, volunteer, or join a soup kitchen. In such cases, the person themselves may not be aware that their gift is being activated for God's business, nonetheless, that is exactly what is happening.

There are some gifts like miracles, healing, prophecy, word of wisdom, and word of knowledge that also operate more efficiently during focused periods of worship. These too may be hard for you to notice but if you pay attention, you can see God enhancing all your spiritual gifts when you worship Him and practice having consistent periods of focused worship with God.

Mature believers are able to identify and refine their spiritual gifts during their quiet time of worship at home and at the corporate worship services on the weekend. Corporate worship however is the best time to engage, and use your spiritual gifts to serve God and help others to serve Him too. I have been blessed with the spiritual gift of intercessory prayer, and when I was young, I would exercise that gift by sitting in my seat and praying for others in the church. Although they were unaware on most occasions that I prayed for them. However, I saw God answer my prayers made on behalf of my fellow church-family members over and over. I was doing God's business by using my gifts to serve other believers. I didn't have to lay my hands on them or be noticed. All I needed was to know my gift and use it as God directed me.

With the proper mentorship, new or untrained believers who worship God intensely are able to start to discover their spiritual gifts. There are many spiritual gifts in the bible all of which I believe can be enhanced during the period of focused worship, which usually takes place in corporate worship or periods of personal quiet time. The gifts of leadership, discernment, help, mercy, administration, and a host of others can all be activated and boosted in focused worship. If you are aware of this and look forward to God activating your spiritual gifts during times of praise and worship, you can learn more about how He wants to use you in the kingdom of God family business.

Worship prepares you to function in the family business. God uses all aspects of who you are and although your spiritual gifts play a large role in what God wants you to do in His business, however, you should open up all areas of your life to be used by the Lord. God will use your character, your personal experiences, your natural talents, your weakness, and your failures if they can help to build the family business.

Although I won't go into much detail on this matter, but God also uses you within the context of a community. Sometimes God allows your local church to collectively serve your community or perhaps organize a mission in another country to spread the love of Jesus Christ to others. Sometimes families are used to accomplish great tasks for the glory of the family business. But the main point I want to make here is that God will connect you to the family business through focused and love-filled worship.

9.

Conclusion

As we approach the end of our journey, I believe that this book has provided you with a wonderful foundation as it relates to building the spiritual skill of worship. Worship much like prayer and bible study is a spiritual skill designed to transform your life. Worship's ultimate priority is to bring you into an intimate relationship with your creator. This relationship impacts you and causes you to grow spiritually. I wish to motivate you to worship God in spirit and in truth by recognizing the five major benefits of worship, as this awareness will inspire you to enter the presence of God with an expectation.

Throughout the book, I have maintained the importance of focused worship with the Lord. It is great praising God while working, while caring for your family, or multitasking, but you should never forget that there is an increased power in focused worship. Like most other Christian authors, I believe that worship is a lifestyle and should be a part of every aspect of our life, however, powerful and life-transforming praise requires focused time with God.

Intimacy with God calls us to pay attention to the Lord. You must spend quality time with Him and have a heart of obedience and faith. The scriptures make it clear that worship requires obedience and for that reason, you must employ the wisdom of the scriptures in your journey of admiration towards God. You are called by God to have focused times of worship to honor and lift up His name. And thou shalt love the LORD thy God with all thine heart, and will all thy soul, and with all thy might (Deuteronomy 6:5).

Personal experience is a vital aspect of worship and you need to challenge yourself so that you can grow in your understanding of God. Mentors are of great importance as they provide you with accountability and can broaden your perspective about worship. Models from the scriptures and history can provide you with proven strategies of worship and can aid you in obeying God and living a life well-pleasing to the Lord.

One of the greatest models of worship in history took place at the beginning of the book of Acts. On the day of Pentecost when the Holy Spirit entered the lives of the followers of Jesus. At the inception of the early church, supernatural events started to take place (see Acts 2)., God continues to do supernatural things in current times, at events centred on focused worship. I spoke earlier about worship being transformed into a fragrance, a teacher, a weapon, medicine, and a family business; all of these benefits of worship are designed to honour God and to serve His purpose.

Focused worship is one of the few times that heaven and earth meet each other. Worship is simultaneously a spiritual and a natural event in which God and humanity have communion with each other. Though you may be lifting your hands and singing aloud while standing in a physical room. Your voice is sounding aloud and producing an unseen sweet-smelling fragrance in heaven. Worship is a fragrance.

Though you may be hearing the music and praising God. If you are spiritually attuned to the voice of God, you will hear His still voice speaking to your spirit and teaching you new and wonderful things. Worship is a teacher.

Though the devil may be attacking you on every side and trying to stop your worship God is fighting for you in the midst of it all, and supplying you with victory. Worship is a Weapon.

Though you may have had a hard and challenging week and feel tired in your body as you sing out to God, the Spirit of the Lord is actively renewing you with energy and hope as you praise His name. Worship is a healer.

Though you may be seeking to give God your worship the Lord in turn gives you insight into your spiritual gifts. He opens up the understanding of your purpose and how you can serve others for His glory. Worship is a supernatural family business.

I was blessed to spend this time with you and I want to encourage you to give the Lord focused and passionate worship.

Manufactured by Amazon.ca
Acheson, AB